We Were the People Who Moved

We Were the People Who Moved

a collection of poetry

by

David Ebenbach

TEBOT BACH • HUNTINGTON BEACH • CALIFORNIA • 2015

The Patricia Bibby First Book Prize, 2013
Judge, Ralph Angel

Design and layout: Gray Dog Press, SPokane , WA
Author photo: Marcy Hairston
Cover art: David Guinn

ISBN 10: 1-939678-19-6
ISBN 13: 978-1-939678-19-5
Library of Congress Control Number: 2015944577
1st Edition

A Tebot Bach book

Tebot Bach, Welsh for little teapot, is A Nonprofit Public Benefit
Corporation, which sponsors workshops, forums, lectures, and
publications. Tebot Bach books are distributed by Small Press
Distribution, Armadillo and Ingram.

The Tebot Bach Mission: Advancing Literacy,
Strengthening Community, and transforming life
experiences with the power of poetry through readings,
workshops, and publications.

This book is made possible through a grant from The
San Diego Foundation Steven R. and Lera B. Smith Fund
at the recommendation of Lera Smith.
www.tebotbach.org

For Rachel and Reuben,
who are my actual home

Foreword

Writing fixes the evanescence of sound. It holds it against death.
—Ed Hirsch

Reading David Ebenbach's remarkable debut collection, I thought of Ed Hirsch's dialectic: the always-action of *fixing evanescence,* is, of course, a beautifully fruitless and fruitful enterprise. Like us, poems are made of evanescent stuff; language (sounding) is here and gone. But if death (silence) waits in the wings, a good poem fixes pages with such unexpected sound and sense that we forget, temporarily, all stock endings. Writing and reading, we live a while, delighted. In *We Were the People Who Moved*, David Ebenbach's poems ply the contested space between motion and fixity while searching, with nuanced grace, for what compels us. These poems are neither arrival nor journey; they narrate forestalled spaces we inhabit fitfully, waiting, perhaps, for fate to kick in. Or for rescue?

> We moved from small apartment to small apartment to large apartment to small, from rental to house and to rental again. We moved from boxes in large, cool shadows of buildings over the smell of Italian bread baking to small, white-paneled huddles on stretches of grass to homes that stood at polite distances from one another….This was not some destiny manifesting itself; we moved back at least as often as we moved forward. Even when we weren't moving at all we were in some sense moving back. The accents changed around us, the speed of the cars, the number of stoplights and demonstrative churches. The bumpers changed stickers. Our son walked on uneven sidewalks and between banks of exhaust-darkened snow.
> ("We Were the People Who Moved")

Ultimately, the force that keeps the speaker's family moving in the title poem goes unnamed, hidden. Is it the American Dream? Is it the death of the American Dream? Ebenbach holds us, and the speaker, in suspense, even as the poem builds by list-making. It hides *and* seeks. (In *Nine Gates* Jane Hirschfield reminds us that good poems do both simultaneously.) Its propulsive tempo is ironic, like the family's unwitting progress toward/from fixed positions: "Even when we weren't moving at all we were in some sense moving back." In the book's most arresting poems, Ebenbach marries deft imagery to passive inversions that keep us off-balance, tilting at the edge of revelation. In "You Can't Choose Your Place," human action is portrayed as happenstance while nature rules the day: "Across the street, a dog barks on its own initiative. / A neighbor comes home without a job, / and he leans a sweaty head against his wallpaper and stains it /….This is a moment in your world. / The trees up and down the block make decisions." In "City of Weather," the sky "lies on us with all its weight." In "Mute Love Poem," a skunk killed by a neighbor's dog is "left / in the street, open-eyed in the wide and / bitter aura of its afterlife." But in "High Street," where "there is / no road, in fact, not yet," the poet finds qualified hope in creative action. *Making.* Workmen set bricks "and stand on the edge / of their accomplishment."

> Behind them
> a machine rattles grit down into the cracks.
> It is a hot day in summer, the moon and
> its persuasions very far away. The men
> are not at the edge of anything. They hold the
> street in their hands and then they build it.

Without tricks or trends, guile or self-flattery, without the winking cynicism particular to our age, Ebenbach moves his lines, and his readers, from resonant detail to larger, existential observations with ingenious, clear-eyed authority. His lovely poems grant us momentary stay against silence. Beyond that, they make no promises. I suspect he is at the beginning of a marvelous career.

Dorothy Barresi

Contents

I

II

III

I

We Were the People Who Moved

It was a time of movement, and we were people who moved. We moved from small apartment to small apartment to large apartment to small, from rental to house and to rental again. We moved from boxes in large, cool shadows of buildings over the smell of Italian bread baking to small white-paneled huddles on stretches of grass to homes that stood at polite distances from one another, the sound of lawnmowers and the sound of cicadas crossing our driveways. This was not some destiny manifesting itself; we moved back at least as often as we moved forward. Even when we weren't moving at all we were in some sense moving back. The accents changed around us, the speed of the cars, the number of stoplights and demonstrative churches. The bumpers changed stickers. Our son walked on uneven sidewalks and between banks of exhaust-darkened snow and across lawns and down a street that rarely saw traffic. Were our neighbors moving? We were moving. Though there were times we paused, paused standing on our back decks or on our front stoops or on fire escapes that looked over so many rooftops. It was those moments when we felt it most keenly: the ground under us, already on its way, away.

You Can't Choose Your Place

You can't choose your place.
Across the street, a dog barks on its own initiative.
A neighbor comes home without a job,
and he leans a sweaty head against his wallpaper and stains it
while his wife moves toward him across the floor.
This is a moment in your world.
The trees up and down the block make decisions,
branching this way and that.
Someone on the state road puts up a sign
advertising something you may or may not need.
The sun moves at its pace.
While you stand at your window, in your inevitable place,
a car whose color you did not pick
passes the house.
You thought that might be the one to stop, idle at the curb.
The light shifts out there like a tide.
Even the suitcases by your door,
the bags on the suddenly unfamiliar rug—
you didn't pack those, either.

July Morning

The noise of the cicadas is the day's noise,
swelling into the white light of middle summer
with the smell of the skunk killed in the road
last night. Red cars along the curb, in our
driveways, the asphalt rough with gravel and
gaps. You want to pull a warm leaf from these
weighted trees and taste this morning. Inside
with you, the refrigerator lurches into sound,
calling out, perhaps, for another of its kind.
As are we all.

City of Weather

It's all we talk about here   the way the sky
      lazy after a hot bath
      lies on us with all its weight
We change only to find ourselves damp again
Some weeks the rain comes and stays and leaves
      only to circle back again
      as though looking for lost keys
You'll never find what you're looking for that way
      I think
But the rain persists   interested in lost keys
      but not advice
The ground forgets what it's for
      starts to wander off downstream
There's nothing to hold the sidewalk in place
We close our umbrellas when we can
But here even the sun is a liquid
      sweat on the glass buildings
The night pools around our homes
The night weighs against the apartment windows
And in the morning
We wake as though nothing
      has yet been decided

High Street

The grind of the circular saw squares off
another brick and there is no metaphor—
these dozen men are rebuilding High Street,
bent straight down at the waist to lower it
forward one stone at a time. And if the edge
of the road that's coming to be is angled
like the wash of a wave between the Morning
Sun Café and Phan Shin Restaurant? These
men in their bright tees working at the lip
like sandpipers, sand piled in dunes
ahead of them? Nevermind the inexorable
roll of stone toward College Ave.: there
is no sea between here and there—there is
no road, in fact, not yet, though these men
place their bricks and stand on the edge
of their accomplishment. Behind them
a machine rattles grit down into the cracks.
It is a hot day in summer, the moon and
its persuasions very far away. The men
are not at the edge of anything. They hold the
street in their hands and then they build it.

Space

all around this house, these
many white walls. Out back

the gray swingset fit for a child
of no size, and at the edge

of the far front yard the highway
carries its occasional traffic.

The sky is on every side of everything.

The horizon is the shuddering
of train track, the shuddering

of a line that in the middle
of the night feels all too close—

but in the day it shows us

how far we are from anything.

Departures

The dirt fields alongside the airport
range back in even rows of solar panels
like crops of robot corn.
They open their dark leaves toward the sun,
probably follow it across the sky all day.
Several miles back, tract housing
sits clustered, surprised, in the dust,
while a white marker balloon trails overhead.
Here the panels shine only dully;
they have been built to hold their light.

Richmond, Indiana

The depot only rattles with freight now,
the long exhale of the horn while we sleep
a too-late remembrance, the sound of bells
strained through the screen of time and steady loss.
The old bus station, that bad neon sign
that once peopled the streets with its shadows
has by these days sputtered finally off
and the streets have their even darkness back.
National Road still pushes slow through town,
carrying its cargo of red stop lights,
but the highway three miles north offers up
the elsewhere, the place that's always ahead.
Unless it's us—the elsewhere, the no-place
you can't get to, or even through—just past

City of Oppositions

When does a city eat itself?

Can it go on like this,
blizzard giving way to rain,
then something like spring, all in a week?

Everyone on the street is black
or white.

Even after centuries of hammering all this
into the ground
there's no reason to be sure about any of it.

I am without location
in this place.

After the Ice Storm

the shatter-limbed trees
point to their roots
with extra fingers,
the unharmed branches low,
everything in a crouch
on the clear, hard ground.
On this morning after the ice storm
the trees, like the rest of us,
show their white wood in places
where they've been broken.
We have been warned—
even beauty bears down on us.
Everything struggles
under the weight
of grandeur's
burden.

Tisha B'Av

They've torn the skin off my street. Underneath are the long striations of muscle tissue, but petrified; it seems possible that the city underneath us is essentially dead, that the sewage in its veins moves only for show. It might also be possible, in a long-suffering universe that reaches so casually from here to there, that the city underneath is just an old body moving on geologic time, and that I am impatient, that I am a tiny frenetic beating against the windows of life. Meanwhile this afternoon's rain fills the striations and pours up dirty against the curb, where things are easier; meanwhile on either side of the street scaffolding rises up against the sides of these buildings bone by bone and hangs on, and then at some point each structure comes down, all the ligamenture for just an hour in shining piles along the sidewalks. The advantage then is the sky; maybe I am walking with a book once the rain has stopped and then I realize I am blinded by the pages, and I look up through what I remember to be planks, and there it is—the fringes of the universe, soaked in some kind of blue.

Limits

Here is the problem: Given two ordinary lines in open space,
it's possible for one of those lines to curve toward the other
without ever reaching it. But this is only the nature of limits,
and not the problem. The problem is that the lines are not lines
but bodies, two, walking half-drunk at night together, closer
than they need to be on this sidewalk, in search of more to drink.
Alongside, trucks roll up Route 15 toward Morrisville. And so
they move out of pure math into physical space, into streetlight
the color of yellow wax. Up ahead, DJ's Corner Store and its
small promises. No—this isn't math, and so math isn't the
problem—and not even geometry or physics. No—the problem
is the line, the weakness of the line of the body: how readily it
lunges off parallel. How he does. What forces can explain it?
There is gravity, sure, and loneliness, her sudden beauty and
the beauty of not, for once, knowing. The space between bodies.
Even in this dim yellow he can see that space between them, no
absence, but something there to be touched, the very corpus
of limit. Is that the pleasure? If so, it's a thin one, and
passing. They push open the door to DJ's, and its old spring
just wants it closed again. Inside, shelves lined with beer, wine,
sandwiches, and hardly any space to move around in. Still—
tonight, aside from their drinks, it's all they're going to hold.

Date Night In Richmond, Indiana

On those nights we dragged Route 40 for
something. There was the Applebee's, best
atmosphere in town, said the readers of the
Palladium Item, where we got appetizers and
desserts; the coffee shop with the okay soup
and the evangelical vibe; the Holiday Inn
basement, that semi-fluorescent bar, hard-
carpeted like an office floor where everybody
smoked.

The idea was to talk but we didn't know
how. I had my new students that you could
only picture and you had our baby, and
all day in an apartment where you couldn't
see out of the windows. You could go
outside, where there was nothing to block the
sun. I walked to work, and back, along that
same broken interstate with the trucks that
shouted and the dead buildings; even the
army recruiter had gone out of business. We
wanted somewhere none of it was happening
except us.

But we weren't happening. The Mexican place
where the walls were bright with amateur
murals, and the booth seats raised, like
an illustration of festive—we sat there
one date night and fought again, eating
their chips and ketchup salsa. The waiter
didn't come around until we got quiet. We had
to stop; there was nowhere else to go but back.
I watched the wall of windows, the red of cars
passing behind you.

Sometimes we were happy after. Sometimes
we'd hold hands in the parking lot and agree
what the problem was. Either way it was back
to Route 40 and its flickering box stores, and
just off that the streets of that neighborhood
where there was nothing to block the night and
so we had to drive into it.

Gutters

Again the gutters fill with leaves,
leaves the trees hand down dead
to the sloping rooftop. I spend
today's last hour of light with my
hand in the crackle and sop of it.
Sticks dig my knuckles open. The
breath I get is all mildew. At one
point the ladder swings nearly out
from under me and I hang from
the roof, only the barest foothold
underneath, and the next day the
bruise under my arm will be deep,
right where
I held on.
I work my way around this rented
house, this house at the center of
all this foreign lawn and foliage,
and dig into this muck of leaves.
On the roof beyond my reach are
more leaves, and overhead these
trees, going back on promises or
fulfilling them, ready more leaves
to fall. The roof slopes down. The
gutters are open. In the spot where
I almost fell, the gutter sags just
noticeably, like the mouth of a
person who's right now starting to
understand
something.

Frustrations

The key freezes in the lock;
the steps are narrow;
the clock advances
with the child's voice hotneedling the eardrum.
The pack is heavy with misleading books;
the sun is in a judgmental mood.
The mouth is full of wind and hair,
the belly fat but still hungry;
the ground uneven,
the shoes too loose,
and everything,
the park and street and lot,
grown too thick with the unscalable.

Friday Afternoon in Brooklyn

The siren spreads across Brooklyn and I, so long
in the Midwest, first think it's a severe weather

warning, like the night we found a neighbor's
basement while a tornado moved past

Richmond, Indiana, and we were possessed
by elaborate imaginings of a twister along 4th Street,

but in Brooklyn the siren just means
Shabbat, a warning about

Shabbat. They say it's 100 decibels, same as
a motorcycle or a snowmobile. In Brooklyn

Shabbat is serious, comes at you like summer weather.
Judaism is serious in Brooklyn—when the young

women pedal by in hipster t-shirts, in skirts past
Satmar eyes, the city has to paint over the bike lanes.

And the hipsters have to repaint them
under their videocameras at night. In Brooklyn

youth is serious, and so is the blog. In southwest Ohio
Christianity is serious, the churches with their

signs out front, *No Freedom But In Christ,* or
Don't Make Demands Of God—Await His

Instructions. Even the funny ones—*To Avoid Burning,*
Apply Son-Screen—even the Touchdown Jesus statue

struck by lightning, not so funny. Once on the ride
between these places, we see a sign—*Your*

Parents Are Lying to You About Santa—and
a phone number to call. Alongside all this, another farm.

Farms everywhere, advertising McDonald's, milk,
God in various forms. We drive the landscape

at illegal speeds, serious about getting through.
For those two days, the car is our place, like

the invented under-the-bed country of a child.
Radio static, road noise; Ohio becomes Pennsylvania

becomes New York, where old traffic thunders and we
step stunned into another space. Fold out couch,

guest room, childhood bed reclaimed. Windows
over Brooklyn, the people walking, the BQE,

the delivery trucks. All the urgent tasks of the day.
In Ohio the freight trains howl over the towns and

fields every morning. Now, in the air—it's all
summer out there, all sun, no sign of storm

or the end of the day—the siren stops after
maybe a minute. People take off their aprons,

bring down their stores' metal shutters or
don't. Clean their stations for closing or

don't. They've heard the siren. They head home
if they're going to, or turn their eyes

back to their work. In any case they step
toward something. Everyone has decided

what to do next; everyone knows what's coming.

Ha Lachma Anya

Each day, just for the exercise, I do this walk:
a half-hour of Richmond and its quiet everything.
I don't look at it. I read my book, glancing up
only enough to be sure there are no cars coming.
There are no cars coming. I'm reading Jane Kenyon,
have been reading Kenyon and reading me as well,
and thinking that both of us need some leavening.
Jane, I've been thinking about the way you rhyme,
only toward the poems' ends, and hidden, like a deer
with its vulnerable head nosing between the trees.
Still—there's a feint toward order in that universe.
My nose, of course, is stuck in your poetry,
and so while men sit smoking outside the factory
and two people unload their old station wagon,
while a long ladder rides up a telephone pole,
I have my own world. You're in it, Jane, and me—
I'm thinking of Passover, how by the second night
my guts were already in the Taskmaster's fist,
as though they were filled with mortar
and sharp corners, as though I'd had a double portion
of that bread of affliction for many months or years.
I sat at the shortened table of the second seder
and ate only what matzah was required of me—
a *k'zayit*, a fragment of hard flour the size of an olive—
while the kids around us complained about everything
like full-grown experts. One of the greatest problems
concerning the Passover holiday is keeping kosher,
says a Jewish website. But I was talking about poetry.
Poetry and how despite that creeping rhyme,
your next poem always falls into entropy again.

22

If you were walking through Richmond, Indiana,
you'd be missing your birches and your dark pines.
It's been weeks since Passover and still I often flinch
when I turn my thoughts toward the next meal:
can I eat that? They say *chametz*, leavening, is evil,
you know, and then let us eat it most of the year.
But I've been reading my own stuff, too, Jane,
and I think I've been steering too clear of that evil.
Say I did look up at the liquor store by the bridge—
what would I see there? Generations of townies
fallen further into the glass, a dirty white sign
advertising what we already know is on the shelves.
Where is the rising in me, that rising vision?
Everything around us might expand, might split
open to reveal some truth that isn't exactly hidden.
But if you are unleavened, can you be leavened?
I keep up my walk, eyes cast down onto your pages,
my gut ready to clench with the next affront.
You write about a pear with a secret rotting inside.
Meanwhile, the bridge spans high over some small wet,
and so, unchanged, I cross the water without parting it.

Birds, Et Cetera

I'm going to write a memoir,
just as soon as I get it together
and start appreciating life.
You know, the beautiful things:
birds, et cetera. Flowers and
what not. When I can hardly
walk a block without stopping,
wading through my own awe
at every blade of earnest grass.
Right now I mostly notice how
the grass breaks the sidewalk
as it forces its way into the open.
Or the way my wife goes allergic
when flowers pop up around us.
Or the bird shit, quite frankly,
that streaks the door of my car
right where my hand wants to go
to close that door. And then
I think about how so many people
have worked so hard to get a car
but don't have anywhere to go,
and just want to drive around,
and now they've got a handful
of excrement, and nobody's hand
to shake anyway. And that's why
the memoir has got to wait.

II

Things We Can Be Sure About

Certainly our mother
put plastic bags around our feet
before we stepped into boots.

We pointed our toes into the sharp corners,
as though the bags were carefully shaped for feet,
but our heels were loose in plastic space.

And then our feet stayed dry,
aside from our own sweat,
which left our skin dead and white.

The snow outside was high,
standing over us like grownups
on either side of a shoveled path.

Certainly we were wary of snowballs,
which required aim,
and raised the body's fear of ice.

But the hallway out to the front door
was dark and taller than any grownup,
haunted even in full-on daytime.

Certainly we knew what meant what
as we stood in the vestibule on overinsulated feet,
between the snow pushed up against the porch
and the heat of the well-known house.

Three-Card Monte

Back of the 42 bus, in the big shade of the rear doors—
the same doors kids hopped for free rides—sometimes
there was a guy with three cards overturned on a *Daily
News* in his lap. I remember the backs were red, and when
he faced them up they were black, clubs, with just one
queen. Under the hollow of his hands she juked side to
side, jumped like double dutch, ran off, and—in the
demonstration rounds—came right home, smiling. But
after that, unless the shill was playing, she left with money
and came back with an abundance of promises. Not that
I knew what was happening then; all I knew was my own
blank terror as his eyes pressed around for customers. He
even wanted to know if I had any cash, but I was a kid
and all I had in my pockets were my hands. So one day
he demonstrated on me, and though my finger shook as
I pointed he made sure the white boy was a winner
every time. Then back to the grownups, and me watching
for free again, sort of. The cards popped and hissed and he
barely seemed to touch them. What really stayed with me
were the times when he seemed to slip, mishandled the cards
so that the queen was bent at the corner, and the way she
turned up again healed, having handed off the injury
to one of the number cards. I don't know what awed me
the most—the bending he let you see, or the bending he
didn't, or the sense, even though I had nothing to lose,
of danger: that he could take something from me, something
I didn't know I had, even if he had to slip it to me first.

Private School

First through fourth,
somehow.
I took a train to the suburbs.
My Mom at work, of course,
I walked myself to the station
deeper into the neighborhood—
through the unknown on the map,
the There Be Monsters part.
    (One time,
    an old man lying in the street
    between parked cars,
    the running blood
    the only color on his face,
    his arm up for help.
    Another time,
    a kid, bigger than me,
    pointing a broken bottle.
    You'd better run, he said.
    I did run, then—
    I remember my winter coat
    not fitting
    on my churning body,
    my backpack leaping.
    In fact, I ran both times.
    I left the old man there, too,
    with his nightmare blood.)
On the other end of the tracks
one of those old mossy stations
that waits quietly for the trains,
and the uneventful walk to school.

Every Thursday,
silent meeting in the mornings.
I didn't know what to think about.
The teachers stood up
with their morality stories.
In the only one I remember,
two mice struggled
to get cheese from a stick,
teetering on the lip of a bucket.

Snowfall

This is the rain that won't
leave us, that in the morning
will still be here, curled up

against our car tires and trees,
our homes, thick in the grass,
deep the length of the sidewalk.

This is the naïve rain that
thinks it can break the cycle,
live here quietly among us.

This is the rain that believes it's permanent—
and only because of the children,
who mark it everywhere with angels.

Shabbat Comes Over West Philadelphia

Shabbat comes over West Philadelphia
on quiet wings. As the sun heads off into
the higher numbers, up from Center City
comes the night. Street lights hum on.
Cars click slowly into spots on this block
or the next while someone stretches out
on a bench in Clark Park, the ongoing
sound of the basketball not a rhythm but
a cadence. Dinner time comes to kitchen
after kitchen. People go in to their food
and television, and those who come out
again take to the steps for an evening of
nothing much. They watch that nothing
much. It never gets all the way dark here,
the light is the orange grease they pop
corn in at the movie theater, but it's dark
enough that faces go over to further and
further shadow. Buses and trolleys. It all
continues, slower and slower, until the
only things moving are the raccoons, the
stray cats, the young men unable to rest.
One kid gets dropped at home very late.
Out of the car, up the porch steps to the
front door. The sound of keys loud on a
stilled street. He goes in without having

noticed Shabbat moving down Osage Avenue. He wouldn't know how to find the sound of angels within the sound of traffic remote on another street, the buzz of the streetlight, the cadence of the heart. But he will.

What Work It Is

I decided to live on my wits.
Philip Levine

But when does a kid realize it—that his wits are
something he can live on? That they aren't just
a middle-school liability—that he has food in his
head, and a house in there, and work that doesn't
kill a person, and probably love? When does he
find that bright coin in the break in the sidewalk
broken the length of his street, and know he has
something he can spend? What does he feel in his
back, bending away from his mother to pick it up?
And when he stands—the old row homes fading
banks of fog, and behind them the first dark shapes
of his actual given life—

Setting Out

At seventeen I had no sense of the country,
had never been further west than Pittsburgh,
and so when we crossed into Ohio to look
at colleges, the land spread out flat as if to say,
This is another place altogether. Only the south
of the state, with its willingness to hill,
seemed familiar, but I didn't end up there—
in a year I'd be forty-five minutes outside of
Cleveland. The landscape was a kind of vacuum,
a kind of outer space; two thousand miles
short of California, I in my quiet intersections
thought I saw the edge of the universe. When
it got cold, at night I could get Philadelphia's
news on the AM dial, stray waves across the
atmosphere. It was, say, thirty degrees in Center
City, twenty-eight out at the airport. There,
people boarded planes to somewhere difficult
to imagine. I didn't see them—there were no
planes in our part of the sky, along with no
buildings, no landmarks, no maps of what
had been discovered—only sky, fathomless sky.

The sun in three places

1.
Peach in the tree limbs,
almost unnoticed,
ripe over my shoulder.

2.
Then hot through the glass,
on my neck hot,
this pointed question.

3.
Everywhere, finally—
the sky, glazed across,
the air we're breathing,
our least obvious thoughts.

Getting By

At boring jobs I used to calculate
how much I made per minute, keeping track
of the day, twelve cents by twelve cents, as it
deposited its small worth in the bank.
Once, doing temp work, I passed this along
to my equally bored supervisor,
who did her own math, compared it to mine,
and stomped off to the office manager.
She came back with a raise, and somehow I
wasn't fired. We got back to the work of
ordering envelopes by zip code, by
a labor of something other than love.
A labor of minutes, and here's the thing
about minutes: they just keep on passing.

Poem for a Job that No Longer Exists

It was down in the meatpacking district,
this art gallery owned by a rich guy,
all baldness and tasteful suits, and run by
a lean woman, not his wife, whose manic
energy—part temper, part her frantic
and clearly doomed passion for the rich guy—
redounded, clamored, shattered off the high
white walls. For sure no one ever thanked her.
Me, I manned the phones, and one day got a
series of prank calls: silence on the line.
"It's his wife," my boss said, chewing her thumb
before she fled. Ringing echoed off the
white walls until my plea into the phone
for some mercy: "I'm just the freaking temp."

Lunch

Two women and two men come in, take the table next to me, very close by. I can barely see the men, on my side of the table, but the woman nearest me is long and the other woman stares at her fingers on the tabletop. Then, while her friends talk and work with their menus, the distracted woman breaks away from her fingers, says, *You know what? I was on the subway the other day with this man who was deaf and blind. Deaf and blind. He had to wear a sign around his neck, so you would know that there was no way even to talk to him. How did he know what stop to get off?* One of the men suggests that he could count the stops. *But what if it stops between stops?* she persists. *Sometimes they do. How would he know what was real?* The other man *mms*, for lack of anything better. *I mean, you couldn't even talk to him*, she says. The long woman nearest me finally checks in and says, *I know. I saw a blind man on a subway once, and I wondered how he knew. They don't always announce the stops out loud.* But the other woman, the one who started all this, says, *But no—I mean, this guy was deaf and blind both. You couldn't even tell him anything. Not anything.* She's holding her exasperated menu up in the air.
The waitress comes then, asks if they need more time, but they don't, unexpectedly. Everyone orders something—even the woman who can't let go of the man on the subway has her mind made up about eggs. When the waitress is gone, there is still this pause around the two men and two women. The long woman says, *This place is really cute.* The two men agree. Their troubled friend nods, gets back to the business of her fingers. Now she makes them into signs against the table, signs she seems to have invented.

After a substantial meal, at a performance of the Jazz at Lincoln Center Orchestra

and
these saxophones
glitter
like
so much honey
in the bowl
of this our spoon

Candidate

I've been thinking a lot about life, and you're a good candidate,
I thought I heard my wife say; it was over the phone,
roughed up by distance and the funny way she said it.
Actually she'd said, *and you're a good part of it,* which was
nicer to hear, really, but by the time that got cleared
up I had already made the journey, wondering about
myself, whether I was, really, such a good candidate
for being alive, for living a life, and what I had ever
done to bolster my qualifications—I did take the time,
the other day, to see the light off the yellow reflector
on a neighbor's car—and then I wondered at all the
years I'd put in by then—always one more test, one
more epiphany, one more valid form of identification—
what it takes to declare your candidacy, and to pursue
it: every morning, again, the arduous and infinite nature
of the application process.

The first flowers of one of the final springs

After I gathered up everything from my desk, including my sense of shock, I dumped my stuff in the trunk of the car and drove to a city park where I sometimes liked to eat lunch. It was cold but not too cold. Either way I didn't want to go home. I hung my tie on a bush and walked until I found a bench across from some early spring flowers—yellow, something like trumpets. God was already there on the bench, watching the flowers Herself. I sat down. God, I saw, was a teenaged girl with glasses, chewing on a clump of Her own hair. Her frame was all bone. "They're *so* beautiful, it's awful," She said. I didn't say anything back. I didn't have anything important to say to anyone, and least of all to God. "It's the weirdest to be in these, like, downhill centuries here," She said. "When it's sort of horrible and sort of awesome." I nodded. She was wearing a t-shirt with the word *tzimtzum* on it. I felt for Her, so skinny. "What sucks," She said, "is knowing exactly when it's going to blow up." I looked around at the world, the flowers bobbing their heads like trumpeters side by side in a big band. "When?" I said. She looked at me with unbelievably bright eyes, rolled them. "As if," She said, though not unkindly. "Right," I sighed, and turned my eyes down to my shoes. I scuffed them against the paved path. Soon I was going to have to go home and tell my wife what had happened at work. "I'm totally bumming you out, right?" God said. I shrugged. "I'm sorry," she said. "I'm just like blah, blah, blah." "It's okay," I said. She said, "I had to talk to *someone.*" "Sure," I said. "I understand." When she sighed, I looked Her way. Then She smiled a small implausible smile and stood up off the bench and stretched, all too-skinny midriff, and made a little bashful shrug and scuffed off with Her hands in Her pockets.

The flowers, I saw, all turned their trumpets in Her direction for a moment. But then they came back, and nodded at me, one after the next. Any minute, I thought, some of these flowers are going to start playing music.

Looking For a Job

What you want, at least, is the dignity
of a Sisyphus—you want to see yourself
on a hilltop, your muscles and hands
afire and chest roaring for breath, and
that boulder and its pounding descent
seen at least through your memories
of the throne. But the elevator hauls
you to another unstoried floor, another
hard carpet trod by the many, and your
one suit has a stain at the shoulder, and
you carry your account along the hallway
with the growing sense that it weighs
nothing at all. What weighs, really, is
the fear that this is your myth, this drag
up the hill with empty, tender hands,
and the ride back down again—untold
by gods or men how, during the slow
fall, you take off your suit jacket and
pick at the stain until it becomes a hole.

What We Write About When We're Not Writing Poetry

The whole world is a very narrow bridge,
and the essential thing is to not be afraid at all.
Rabbi Nachman of Bratslav

I am going to put some track lighting up in here,
and train the beams on various concerns:
water damage, social awkwardness, deadlines.
I am going to follow them around like search lights
raining down from the guard towers. We need a new
floor. We might as well get ourselves on automatic
bill pay while we're at it. Do you understand how
serious this is? I have a list that spools out of a slot
between two ribs. And so let's get some light on this:
it's possible we should sell the house and move,
or at least find an open-minded publisher and eat
a little bit better. The showerhead, the five-year-plan—
they need to be replaced. There are these interviews.
The light floods a landscape of dirty dishes, always.
Every morning, the sun over a crusty plate; every night,
the sun behind a clouded glass. We could really use
a filtration system, or at least a filing system, when
you get down to it. But hold on: there aren't enough
paper clips to even get started, and we need more light.
Always more light.

Belly

I finally notice it at a dinner party,
the way it stretches my shirt,
its urgency from the cake I've eaten,
its nerdy gurgles all the way home.

My wife has noticed it, too.
She eyes it from her side of the bed.
My belly is new topography for us. She says,
You really should do something about that.

I take it by car to the doctor's office,
sit among other people with wrong-sized parts;
there is a swollen hand in the lap next to me,
a puffy face staring at me over the magazines.

When it's my turn, the doctor examines my roundness
as though an explorer determined to map me;
there may be an alternate route to the Indies
laid out somewhere on these curving new lines.

Eventually, the doctor relaxes on the rolling stool,
assures me that everything will be all right in time.
It seems that I have merely eaten too much.
If I just eat less, the doctor assures me, the gut will shrink.

At the dinner table, my wife and I discuss the situation.
She agrees with the doctor. I nod, but I'm not so sure.
I eat my normal amount of dinner though we talk about changes,
about reduced portion size and exercise and a long, long life.

Then I wash the dishes contemplatively with my belly against the sink.
The air, in the kitchen and out the open window, is a fog of spices;
everywhere is the rising scent of this city and beyond.

In the Garden of the Presbyterian Historical Society

Three stone men, slightly giant,
stand ankle-deep in a mess of leaves.
Each one is composed of stacked blocks,

the bold seams at the shoulders, the hips—
as if to say: *this part is devoted to your contemplation;*
below that, the terrible gut and heart, the organs of our survival;

and this last, for standing,
as we must,
on the uneven surface of Your world.

The Fine Print

And that's when you discover
that pleasure has always been on loan:

only once you're deeply in debt.

There's no way to pay it all off now.
They come in a white trailer to repossess:

first the soft, pillow-backed couches,
then the tubs of sour cream.

The late nights are no longer yours
to do with as you please,

nor perhaps that untroubled optimism
with which you'd stomped your wild path.

Certainly you lose the salt.

Delight by delight they strip your house,
fill the trailer with fats and anonymous sex.

What can you do but watch from the
unforgiving kitchen chair that's been left you?

They could hurt you, these repo men,
could fill your body with stones.

Kneecaps? They could lay you out flat.

But it's professional, impersonal, all this,
and afterward the driver gets out of the trailer,

walks you around your house with a clipboard,
pointing out what they haven't touched:

a checkbook, a job offer, a child's report card.
At the bottom of the clipboard

is a dark line for your signature.

Sparrows

The sparrows gather nearby,
their anxious heads jerking
every which way.
Someone has taught them
to bring their hunger here,
without quieting their terror
of everything that moves.
And so, having little choice,
they land on the awful perch:
at their feet, all the food in the world,
and just beyond, all the teeth.

We Are All On the Edge of Something

Your house, there on the street
that bends like an elbow, its
sleeve the first trees of a larger
wood; this train that runs along
a drop to the road. Miles now
from my father's home, the city.
The buildings start to crack.
Even the sun, there at the
fingertips of the winter-ready
trees—it stays, as if afraid
to be let go.

Here in the City of Monuments

Here in the city of monuments we make our home among
the stones we've hewn in our image, in the spaces we've
left open. The buildings squat the length of city blocks.
But in this place the shadows are all figurative, and
the streets fill with light, with wind and the slow talk of
edifices. We built them, after all, to speak of us. Yet
in the day above our small movements we sense a larger,
longer conversation, one we can't quite hear, living
between syllables. At night we withdraw our traffic and
these children of ours, old now, stay up still talking about
history and mutual esteem. These towers reach past us.
In our hands, the loneliness of gods.

The Poem is Interrupted

My son enters the poem
forcefully. He is four years
old and has no time for
the landscape I've been
building with the patience
of a bonsai grower: no time
for the row homes, each
one with a different color
paint on the porch roof,
no time for the predictable
split in the sidewalk slate,
no interest in the long road
from that place to this,
one preaching billboard after
another. He shoves aside
the familiar nouns and
replaces *remember, search,*
and *long* with verbs of his
own: *show, give, have.* In
his hands are a clutch of
erasers, which for now he
will keep in a drawer in
the living room. And now
there's an end table in the
poem, a drawer that closes
and opens.

And So You Arrive

And so you arrive,
ancient-faced houseguest,
like some relative out of a sepia-toned photograph,
surrounded by a thousand pounds
of duffel bags and steamer trunks,
the contents spilling loose down our front steps.
Nevermind that we invited you;
nevermind the months of notes we received about your coming;
still your arrival is a surprise.
Maybe we thought it had all been a joke,
a crazy thing we'd dreamed up,
the two of us in some restaurant,
dawdling chatty over the bill,
What would it be like if...?
Now we step past you onto the stoop,
look up and down the street,
which is just a few cars and sidewalk,
looking for someone to ask *Is everyone sure about this?*
There are no confirmations, no explanations
between the bumpers,
along the length of the concrete.
We go back into the house.
Inside, you have already spread your things
in a thin layer across the floor.
Mounds of clothes,
your arcane devices of entertainment.

There's no real time for explanations anyway—
where are our manners?
You must be cold;
you must be hungry;
you must need something.

The ABCs of Parenting

A baby comes;
drop everything.
Forget goals,
however indispensible.
Judge knowledge lightly.
Meekly, now:
open primers,
quote,
recycle seriously
the usual vertiginous
welcome:
xylophone, yellow,
zebra.

A Fall

Trees take after Eve, leaves after Adam,
scattering Eden wide,
the landscape loose with bright color,
while the wood is all bare limb, now—though,
finally, a nudity haloed in fire, with nothing like shame at all.

Shavuot

In this year of infancy,
revelation comes to father and son
in the synesthesia of a thunderstorm.
We stand at the door,
our senses confused by the flashing,
the beating of the air against earth,
the crack of rain on a neighbor's awning.
The boy sees it all for what it is:
another of the many beginnings of life.
He smells the purpling of the atmosphere,
hears ozone left burning all around us,
watches the drumming on all surfaces.
He takes it in the same way he takes everything—
the striped light through the blinds,
the always unexpected mooing of a toy,
Dad's reappearance overhead in the morning—
How about that? he says to everything.

Mute Love Poem

I don't know what to say about the skunk
that our neighbor's dog killed and left
in the street, open-eyed in the wide and
bitter aura of its afterlife, about the city
coming to shovel it off the asphalt but
leaving a lot of the smell behind somehow,
or about the electrical charge of need that
cicadas have been adding to the air all
week, or about the black ants that cross
the bathroom floor on the diagonal,
or what it all has to do with you in a car,
driving the length of Pennsylvania to
come home, come home, all of us right
here, in this place, finally come home.

Harvest

electrical
towers
fold their
long linen
to the
far end
of the
fields
over the
dogs trotting
through
the stubble
while birds
flock
to the
roadside
no longer
a line
along the
asphalt
but a
milling
crowd
back into
the field
under the
electrical
towers
and the

sudden
open hand
of
sky

Pastoral

My boy, aged four, is in the backyard,
breaking open black seed pods to plant
the seeds—he calls them bird beans,
because he's decided birds like to eat them—
and he's wearing a Superman cape,
a cape that doesn't particularly flap or flutter
as he, shuffling—sneakers with no socks—
carries his blue watering can between the yard
and the kitchen sink, the sink where I'm
washing dishes at the window that looks out
at the yard, ready at the seemingly bottomless tap.

To Whom It May Concern

They have built a tree outside my window.
They have built another one behind that.
They have filled both with white flowers,
white like fresh paper, with a little yellow
at the core, for dignity.
The brown limbs underneath the white
are like us. They hold everything up, up.
I write to you about this not to complain—
no-one seeing this could think to complain—
but because someone must mention the trees,
and because someone must need to be told.

Reid Hospital: The Stairs to Psychiatric Services

worn concave
by many feet,

Richmond's shoes
carrying all this
lost stone—

up into
the hallway
of closed doors;

out into
the parking lot
after.

The streets,
the sidewalks
then
marked with this;
rocky with the
black grit of

our

reluctant
upward
steps—

Mural

for David Guinn

On your wall
the moon fat and low
a belly slung against an old undershirt
and oh
what a kindness
to give us a heaven that has
      like us
eaten too much

Rosh Hashanah

Sun pours into the clearing
through the forest's broken roof
and the gnat
as it wanders
becomes the movement of light—
some wavering piece of the above
here among us
as light—
a flare released by an unsteady hand
in the reach of the unsteady heart

Hallelujah

They've torn the fields down,
the thick run of empty stalks
harvested for I don't know what.
For the good of the sky, maybe—
the sky that's kept its distance
all through the growing season.
Now in the great open,
the sky rests on the bristling soil.
This is a new way, a good way,
for us to be alone here.

Oldenburg, Indiana

Even with all these uncounted spires
there's still so much sky—enough to
see weather massing miles from here
like dark hillsides at the horizon, ample
time to joke about what those clouds
are doing to the people in Waynesburg
or Batesville, how much rain is falling
on rival high schools, before it ever
gets here. And when the storm drums
the only surfaces you've ever known
well, you see the end of it coming from
equally far off—and then you've got all
the time in the world to watch it move
on toward Brookville, Metamora, not
so big, those clouds, no more than a
caravan of dark cars with out-of-state
plates driving slow down Main Street,
something to mention to Jim or Meryl
next time you see them, which is today.

Souciance

*The cicada has represented insouciance
(i.e. nonchalance or indifference) since
classical antiquity.*
                    Wikipedia entry

What indifference? The heat of the day
shivers with their calling, each one to
another, and though the branches of the
trees seem unbowed, their noise is the
weight and the breadth of the rising
morning. And if the ant is busy gathering
for the winter, the ant has it easy. There
is no division of labor among the cicadas—
each one has to do it all. And so they
take to the branches, opening up the
wood for their breakfast, calling out
for mates in the ecstatic heat. Under
them the ants do their jobs, and wave
after wave of sound breathes out from
the trees. The day opens wider, the sun
burning like everything else.

Autogeography

Finally, the body is littered with landscapes,
the brain all map and diligent chart.

The three-story row houses line up like memories
over the barbershops and the gas station
along a street grooved with trolley tracks.

A town at the center of a stubbled cornfield
blinks under an unnecessary stoplight,
waits in bone for the winds to come at dark.

There are two lakes breathing in the chest,
one north and large, the other south and smaller,
freezing over each year, but still breathing,

the avenues rough with fleets of gypsy cabs,
the bus idling in front of the YMCA,
the national road with its angry pickup trucks.

There is so much soil in the creases of the skin,
feet black with asphalt, toughened by brown glass.

Finally, the wanderer will settle into one place,
laying the back's weight on the pavement.

The world will take root—
the world will be buried in that place.

Acknowledgements

Many, many thanks to Mifanwy Kaiser and Tebot Bach for shepherding *We Were the People Who Moved* from manuscript to book. I'm grateful to Dorothy Barresi for selecting this manuscript for the Patricia Bibby Prize. It's great to be part of Tebot Bach.

Thanks, too, to the editors at the various literary magazines where some of these poems first appeared: *Artful Dodge, Beloit Poetry Journal, Boxcar Poetry Review, The Collagist, Crosscurrents, DMQ Review, Hawai'i Pacific Review, Hayden's Ferry Review, Iodine Poetry Journal,* the *Journal of the American Medical Association, Killing the Buddha, Literary Mama, morpheme, Oxford Magazine, Phoebe, Poet Lore, Poetica, Sow's Ear Poetry Review, Stirring, Storyscape, Subtropics, Sweet, Thrush Poetry Journal, 2River View,* the *Washington Post, Work, Zeek,* and the anthology *What Poets See* (FutureCycle Press). Some of these poems were also published in my chapbook *Autogeography,* published by Finishing Line Press.

In addition to these many excellent editors, I owe a huge debt to wise and generous friends who helped me develop these poems and this manuscript: Ali Shapiro, Kim Cope Tait, and my most crucial reader, Jaimee Kuperman. I'm also grateful to the Virginia Center for the Creative Arts, where I spent a very productive residency that helped me to finalize this manuscript. Above all, these pages would be blank if not for the longstanding support of my family, and in particular my wife Rachel and my son Reuben, who—language can't handle them. They're just that amazing.

TEBOT BACH
A 501 (c) (3) Literary Arts Education Non Profit

THE TEBOT BACH MISSION: advancing literacy, strengthening
community, and transforming life experiences with the power of poetry
through readings, workshops, and publications.

THE TEBOT BACH PROGRAMS
1. A poetry reading and writing workshop series for venues such as homeless
shelters, battered women's shelters, nursing homes, senior citizen daycare
centers, Veterans organizations, hospitals, AIDS hospices, correctional
facilities which serve under-represented populations. Participating poets
include: John Balaban, Brendan Constantine, Megan Doherty, Richard Jones,
Dorianne Laux, M.L. Leibler, Laurence Lieberman, Carol Moldaw, Patricia
Smith, Arthur Sze, Carine Topal, Cecilia Woloch.

2. A poetry reading and writing workshop series for the community Southern
California at large, and for schools K-University. The workshops feature
local, national, and international teaching poets; David St. John, Charles
Webb, Wanda Coleman, Amy Gerstler, Patricia Smith, Holly Prado, Dorothy
Lux, Rebecca Seiferle, Suzanne Lummis, Michael Datcher, B.H. Fairchild,
Cecilia Woloch, Chris Abani, Laurel Ann Bogen, Sam Hamill, David Lehman,
Christopher Buckley, Mark Doty.

3. A publishing component to give local, national, and international poets a
venue for publishing and distribution.

Tebot Bach
Box 7887
Huntington Beach, CA 92615-7887
714-968-0905
www.tebotbach.org